PARIS

SECRETS

PARIS
SECRETS

ARCHITECTURE • INTERIORS • QUARTIERS • CORNERS

Text and principal photography by Janelle McCulloch

images
Publishing

Published in Australia in 2009 by
The Images Publishing Group Pty Ltd
ABN 89 059 734 431
6 Bastow Place, Mulgrave, Victoria 3170, Australia
Tel: +61 3 9561 5544 Fax: +61 3 9561 4860
books@imagespublishing.com
www.imagespublishing.com

Copyright © The Images Publishing Group Pty Ltd 2009
The Images Publishing Group Reference Number: 830

National Library of Australia Cataloguing-in-Publication entry:
Author: McCulloch, Janelle.
Title: Paris secrets : architecture, interiors, quartiers, corners / Janelle McCulloch.
ISBN: 9781864703085 (hbk.)
Subjects: Architecture—France—Paris.
               Interior architecture—France—Paris.
               Interior decoration—France—Paris.
Dewey Number: 720.94436

Production by The Graphic Image Studio Pty Ltd, Mulgrave, Australia
www.tgis.com.au

Pre-publishing services by Splitting Image Colour Studio Pty Ltd, Australia

Printed on 140gsm Goldeast paper with 40oz caseboard by Everbest Printing Co. Ltd.,
in Hong Kong/China

IMAGES has included on its website a page for special notices in relation
to this and its other publications. Please visit www.imagespublishing.com.

CONTENTS

INTRODUCTION

'To know Paris is to know a great deal.'

– Henry Miller

What makes Paris so seductive, year after year? What is it about this bewitching city that constantly charms admirers and critics alike, and convinces them to perpetually award it *plus populaire*: destination *extraordinaire*? Is it the glamour and the grandeur – the gracious architecture, inimitable interiors and sophisticated symmetry; all of which are so quintessentially Parisian? Is it the famously majestic avenues with their dignified icons and carefully designed lines of sight? Or is it perhaps the smaller things; those Parisians call *petit trésors*, the small but beguiling treasures of life? Such as the sight of an authentic old neighbourhood bistro, or *troquet*, on a winter's night, with its zinc counter, paper-covered tables and mirror menus reflecting all of the life within. Or the ever-changing window displays of Paris's famous patisseries and tea salons, with their ravishing pastries and delicate cakes packaged exquisitely in fancy *bonbonnière*, like whimsical, sugarcoated *bijouterie* (jewellery). Or the elegant streetlamps of the city's bridges, which throw sentimental light over the cobblestones while the old boats drift beneath, playing the obligatory French tunes from behind. Even the ephemeral aspects of the city, from the dappled, antique-postcard-style light that turns a quiet side street into a Doisneau photograph to the liquid comfort of a cool Kir Royale, drunk while sitting on a woven café chair watching the world go by, remind you that you can only be in one city – Paris. Perhaps it's a combination of both – the fixed and the fleeting; the grand gestures and the gentle moments – that give Paris its richness and spirit? Whatever it is, there is no other city like this. As Henry Miller once said 'the streets sing, the stones talk, the houses drip history, glory, romance …'

If there is one problem with Paris, it is this: the city has a propensity for keeping the best bits to itself. Enchanting courtyards, for example, are often hidden behind enormous carved wooden carriage doors, although a touch of the digicode and a push of the iron doorknocker is often all that's needed to venture within. The quiet neighbourhood gardens, too, are tucked away on streets that are almost deliberately difficult to find, so that discovering them is as much a part of the charm as seeing the cool green oases beyond the gates. Even Paris's most well-known public spaces – the Luxembourg Gardens, the Louvre, the Palais Royal and the Île Saint-Louis – keep their little secrets, sometimes even from the locals.

So how do you discover these quiet corners, set back off the well-trodden boulevards? Well, you can walk the streets, which offer all kinds of unexpected visual treats. As George Sand said, 'I know of no other city in the world where it is more agreeable to walk along in a reverie'. Or you can befriend a Parisian, and charm them into showing you their most relished haunts and hideaways. Or you can take inspiration from the pages to come. *Paris Secrets: Architecture, Interiors, Quartiers, Corners* shows you the insider's Paris: the tucked-away gardens and quiet neighbourhoods squares; the seductive stairwells and winding side streets; the fiercely chic hotels and luxurious, high-ceilinged apartments; and the secret sides of the famous sights, along with the rest of the places that make Paris what it is, including the city's most irresistible cafés, bistros, tea salons and patisseries – each photographed beautifully with architecture and atmosphere shown in spectacular detail.

Part photographic essay, part intimate guide book, *Paris Secrets: Architecture, Interiors, Quartiers, Corners* captures this gracious city in all its light, shade, grandeur and glamour, and shows why so many people surrender to the magic of Paris year after year.

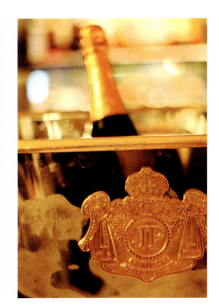

Fellini s'a... ...
avec le... mais... ...lement
ce n'était... très sérieux. Il a... ...
une femme dans... ...a Masina.
elle s'appelait G... ...
Il a vécu cinquante ans
avec elle et ils ont fait
ensemble plusieurs chefs-
d'œuvre : *La Strada, Les Nuits
de Cabiria, Ginger et Fred
et Juliette des Esprits.*

ARCHITECTURE

'To breathe Paris conserves the soul.'

– Victor Hugo

Paris takes its architecture very seriously. Every year, legions of workmen take to the streets to scrub and refresh the city's noted stone façades, continuing a tradition of upkeep that has been part of Paris since Napoleon III demanded it in 1852. If there is one city that knows all about aesthetics, it is this one.

Architecture has always been important to Parisians. It is as integral to their lives as love, lively conversation, well-cut fashion and quality coffee. Ask any Parisian and they'll tell you that a pleasing streetscape is a substantial part of their *qualité de vie* – their famously stylish way of life – not to mention a concrete testament to their finely honed sense of aesthetics. Indeed, for Parisians, if something is not beautifully aligned, be it in their grand boulevards or their petit salons, it can make them quietly distressed.

Much of this awareness can be attributed to one man: Baron Georges-Eugène Haussmann. Arguably Paris's greatest architect, he came to power as prefect under Napoleon III's reign in the late 19th century and set about reforming the city and creating the Paris we know today.

Prior to that time, Paris was a medieval labyrinth and something of an urban catastrophe. Streets were dense, narrow, irregular and interweaving, buildings were inconsistent in size and style, with half-timber houses leaning wearily against each other. Traffic, society and life were utterly chaotic, unsocial and unsanitary as a result of it all.

Haussmann's plan, which was no small one, was to level many of the old streets and redesign a new and more rational urban site; one built on wide thoroughfares, uniformly elegant façades, pleasing lines and sophisticated vistas. It also involved installing water, natural gas and sewerage systems to service an ever-expanding population in hygienic fashion. In short, it involved a complete restructuring of much of the city – more than 85 miles of it.

The new order, he argued, would allow for easier traffic flow – although others murmured that it also prevented rebel barricading and allowed direct gunfire in the event of uprisings – while the tree-lined boulevards allowed the city to breathe, adding grandeur and elegance as they did so.

With the full support of Napoleon, Haussmann set about straightening Paris's main thoroughfares to make navigating easier while linking the boulevards to create cohesion and order. Then he started on the architecture – and this is where the 'new Paris' really started taking shape. New building codes were introduced that corrected and regulated the city's once inconsistent building heights, and rooftop inclines were set to 45 degrees. The heights of the buildings were determined by the widths of the streets, and neighbouring buildings were required to have floors at the same height and aligned façades. As well, the six- and seven-storey buildings had to be built of the best materials using the highest-quality workmanship and feature regularly proportioned windows for unity, balconies for balance, and different doors and details for interest. To keep the order, and perhaps also the peace, Paris's authorities were given power to intervene on the aesthetic aspect of frontages if they felt they weren't in keeping with the new spirit.

Regulations were also imposed on boulevards, public parks and city monuments. Napoleon once said: 'Men are only as great as the monuments they leave behind', and he and Haussmann were certainly determined to leave a memorable legacy.

What ensued, however, was not only memorable, but also wholly harmonious. Paris was unified and defined by its new form, and Parisians realised they were now living in a splendid new city. There was a crisp symmetry to the streets, an effortless grace to the architecture, and a new joy to be had in sitting at the hundreds of new street cafés on the grand avenues, watching the world go by.

The Paris of today is not much different to the Paris of Haussmann's day. His plan for the city was so visionary that few have wanted or indeed needed to change it since. More than a century after it was built, Haussmann's Paris of handsome Neo-Classical façades, elegant, easily navigable boulevards and inviting urban life can still be seen today. The man may have had his critics, but there is no doubt his heart was in the right place.

Paris's famous architecture can be enjoyed at any level – from street to top floor – but to really appreciate it, it is necessary to get out and walk. Walking allows you to experience parts of Paris – the whimsical vignettes, memorable details and magical subtleties – you wouldn't see if you were whizzing around underground or cosseted in the back of a taxi. The mind, not to mention the senses, can absorb a lot more when the body is only going at three miles an hour. Walking – or strolling, as the Parisian gait is much slower than in London or New York – also allows you time to think, to contemplate the city. You can explore it further, like a child lost in a candy store. An open doorway may lead to an impromptu interlude in a startlingly gorgeous courtyard. A side street may beckon with its cobblestone beauty and ornate iron balconies, brimming with ivy and flowers. And a secret park gate may lead to all sorts of unexpected aesthetic rewards.

Walking also allows you to *engage* with Paris, to interact with its architecture and its street life. It is only by wandering the boulevards and lanes that you will really get a feel for the city; and understand its beauty and its rhythms.

The fabric of Paris is made up of many different threads – signs, façades, street scenes, architecture, boutiques, boulevards, parks, gardens and even courtyards. And, just as in a tapestry, each of them is intricately linked to the next in subtle and often almost imperceptible ways. A row of cream stone buildings may be unified by a lacework of Parisian-black, wrought-iron balustrades, while an enclave of stores may be amalgamated by a series of beautifully fine black-and-white signs. There is even one corner of Saint-Germain-des-Prés where a narrow side street leads to a cobblestone pedestrian lane, which leads to a quiet residential courtyard, and then another smaller courtyard, and then a smaller one still; each thoroughfare more delicate and intriguing than the next, but all of them linked by subtle architectural details that make you feel as though you're walking through the urban equivalent of a Russian matryoshka doll. The key to understanding Paris is to follow these threads. Don't worry about where you're going, since you can never get lost in Paris – just set out with your eyes open and your camera at the ready, and you'll be rewarded by some of the most captivating sights you'll ever see.

THE ARCHITECTURE OF ROOFTOPS

The bustling boulevards and quiet side streets are not the only places where you can catch a glimpse of Paris life. Few people realise that there is an entire city that exists above Paris: the city of *dessus de toit* – rooftops and skylines. With fewer of the green parks or sea spaces that you'd find in places like San Francisco, London or Melbourne, Parisians have fashioned another way of escaping their miniscule living rooms: they go outside their windows. Here, amid blue-grey rooftops that start out white in the early light, shimmer like tinfoil in the midday sun and then turn a gentle gold of an evening, they set up their striped deckchairs, kick off their shoes and pour themselves a cool drink, toasting the city before them. If you are ever given the opportunity to visit someone who lives on the top floor of an apartment building, or have the money to book the highest suite at a fancy hotel, it is well worth the hike up the stairs. Because here, overlooking the famous rooftops of the city, you really get a feel for the romantic, old-fashioned Paris; the Paris of *Moulin Rouge* and all the old black-and-white postcards of our childhoods.

THE ARCHITECTURE OF STREETLIGHTS

Paris is known as the City of Light for several reasons. The name was originally in tribute to its intellectual preeminence and all those artists, writers and philosophers who captured the spirit of the city in their publications and paintings. But it is also regarded as the City of Light for its beautiful appearance at night, especially under the beams of streetlamps and spotlights. Paris was one of the very first places to adopt street lighting, and this luminosity, which only added another level of elegance to the already theatrical city, was seen as such a success by the city's chiefs that City Hall eventually set up an entire department to handle this little-known but vitally important issue. Then, just as it is now, the 'Lighting Department' was responsible for not only handling the intensity and timing of the lights but also choosing the design, style and colour of lighting for the 300 monuments, icons and ancient buildings earmarked for illumination. One of these structures is, naturally, the Eiffel Tower, which – apart from New Year's Eve when it explodes with wattage – is lit by more than 20,000 flashing lights that dazzle for 10 minutes

every hour on the hour until 1 am. The lighting of the Eiffel Tower was such a mammoth task, though, that it's a wonder it was ever attempted at all. The project involved dozens of architects, engineers and even mountaineers – for who else was going to climb the iron heights and position the beams? The rest of Paris's buildings and sights are illuminated using strategically placed globes – many of the buildings have lights attached to their sides as well as their fronts in order to highlight their urban curves. Façades that may seem unremarkable during the day can often become dramatic at twilight as a result of this strategic array. Even the stuffiest of public buildings and the most unprepossessing churches and monuments look all twinkly and magic at night. It's a strategy designed to make Paris the most beautiful city in the world, even when the last pink shades of twilight finally sink beyond the Seine and the sky fades from navy-blue to a romantic velvety black. For something different, try seeing Paris at night. You'll be rewarded with a truly heightened sense of Paris's glorious surrounds.

THE ARCHITECTURE OF DOORS Paris is famous for its doors. They are among the glories of French architecture. While places such as Istanbul, Marrakech and Bali may boast impressive entrances, few of them have the variety that Paris has: timber, ornate, enormous, tall, carriage or small; with brass knockers or with iron; with one hinge or five. Used to create a statement of sophistication at the entryway to residences, they are often more elaborate than the courtyards they hide. And indeed, there is nothing like strolling Paris and admiring its doors, wondering if the apartments within are as magnificent as the sentries that protect them. The heavier doors, known as carriage doors, were originally used as protection, sheltering residents from the dangers and unrest of the city outside, but eventually they began to be appreciated for their intricate designs. Today, these doors continue to serve dual purposes. They are extraordinarily beautiful and they still only allow residents and their trusted friends in. In fact, a majority of buildings in the inner city have two doors – an outside street door and an inside courtyard door – and both are armed with digicodes and doorbells respectively. All very private. All very Parisian.

THE ARCHITECTURE OF APARTMENTS The façades and designs of Parisian apartments have changed little since Haussmann's day. If you wander through the Left Bank, and in particular down rue Saint-Sulpice and rue du Four, you'll see many fine examples of Haussmann's style, identified by the standard *hôtel particulier* floor plan. Apartment buildings constructed during the Baron's time included courtyards to provide light and restrict street noise, L-shaped layouts to allow for more light, and exteriors featuring second- and fifth-floor balconies (as these were the two most desirable floors to live on). They also usually included parquet floors, mouldings and fireplaces with marble mantles. Today, these apartments still stand, and are just as beautiful as they were then. Many are also available to rent through agencies such as Chez Vous (www.chezvous.com) for those who wish to live the Parisian life without having a buy a place outright.

Photography supplied courtesy of Chez Vous. www.chezvous.com
Apartment available to rent through Chez Vous

THE ARCHITECTURE OF COURTYARDS

Parisians love a secret, almost as much as they love a beautiful façade, and because of this there are few things they love more than a finely crafted courtyard. They love the sense of privacy courtyards offer and the fact that they are like a 'city within a city': they represent miniature urban oases within the bustling metropolis, a haven from the chaos of life. Indeed, such is their passion for these architectural spaces that the Pavillon de l'Arsenal once presented a show called *Paris cote cours: La ville derrière la ville* (*Courtyards of Paris: The city behind the city*), which revealed some of the city's most extraordinary inner spaces, those that were public and celebrated, and those that were very, very private. For the untutored pedestrian, it can be difficult gaining access to these bewitching Parisian places; often you have to wait until someone invites you, or you discover one by happy chance as one of the residents slips in behind the carriage door just as you're strolling past. It is only then you'll get a glimpse of the architectural riches within: the ivy growing up a stone wall; the iron garden chair resting silently beside a tree; potted geraniums thriving beside a door. Of course, not all of the city's courtyards are technically courtyards. Paris architecture being what it is; a weaving, ever-changing hybrid of façade, street and scene; some of them are really passages, impasses, allées and even streets (such as Avenue Frochet, which is often referred to as a courtyard). Architects today use the word *redan*, or fortification, instead of *cour*, because the term has become so loose in French contemporary language. Whatever they are when they're not pretending to be a courtyard, there is no doubt of their allure. The architect Alexandre Chemetoff once wrote of them: '[The courtyard] shows a hidden city, secret, reserved, in contrast to the strict alignments of boulevards and places.' It is curious that architects love them so much now because for a while, during the mid-century of the

Modernists, they were considered old-fashioned and out of line with contemporary Paris's hard edges and steel forms. Then someone noticed how enchanting they really were and now courtyards are back in favour, although many Parisians protest that they never really went out of fashion. As the courtyard exhibition's curator, Pierre Gangnet, remarked when the exhibition opened: 'Paris is a city of courtyards as others are of towers or parks or water: a transitory space where private and public mingle.' The prettiest courtyards in Paris include the Cour de Rohan in the sixth arrondissement (left), a mysterious, almost magical set of cobblestone passages leading from one courtyard to the next that is so enthralling, it was chosen as the quintessential Parisian backdrop for the famous film *Gigi*, the grand courtyard Helena Rubinstein had built in 1934–7 at 24 Quai de Bethune on the Île Saint-Louis (which, unfortunately, is private), and the secret courtyard (which, fortunately, is public) at the northeast end of the Place des Vosges, set under the colonnade, a world away from the tourists and ball games. There are many, many others too; but much of the beauty and magic of a courtyard is in discovering it for yourself. Go for a stroll around Paris. You'll come across a lovely one soon enough.

THE ARCHITECTURE OF THE HÔTEL CARNAVALET (MUSÉE HISTORIQUE DE LA VILLE DE PARIS)
One of the most beautiful buildings in Paris, and the only 16th-century hotel in Paris that remains intact today, the Hôtel Carnavalet is an astonishingly elegant ode to French architecture at its finest. Originally built for a Parisian politician by the same architect who built much of the Louvre, Lescot, it was designed with utmost attention to symmetry and detail. The original main entrance, situated off rue de Sevigné, gives a glimpse of this symmetry, and an idea of what it must have been like to have alighted from a carriage into this engaging pocket of charm. It would have also been a respite from the tempestuous urbanity of Renaissance Paris: the grand gates and heavy walls offering protection from the frequent unrest of the streets outside. Today, the parterre garden still offers a rest, but only from the exhaustion of seeing the exhibits – which fittingly, show a history of Paris – displayed in the museum within.

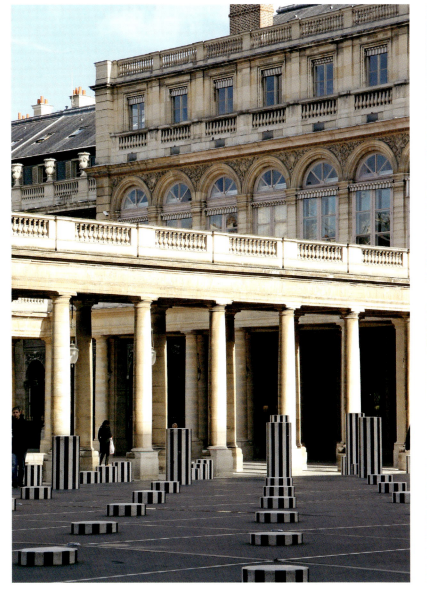

THE ARCHITECTURE OF THE PALAIS ROYAL One of the grandest of the world's squares, next to the Place des Vosges, which is situated nearby, and the prototype for the urban European square, the Palais Royal has the feel of a well-appointed salon, and is beloved as an 'exterior living room' by Parisians and visitors alike. The garden and palace – although it wasn't a palace for long – is noted for several features: the famous forecourt (*cour d'honneur*) peppered with black-and-white columns, the elegant colonnades that surround the garden, which shelter some of Paris's finest shops and restaurants, including Le Grand Véfour, and the grand design of the garden itself, with its perfect rows of pleached lime trees and welcoming quiet. The buildings have been home to, among others, Louis XIII's mother, the Queen-Mother Anne of Austria, the young Louis XIV and Louis XIV's brother, Philippe. But the Palais Royal has also been home to brothels and various casinos, which were lodged in second-floor quarters. Few of the royals and the rebels remain. The Palais Royal is now a haven for the wealthy middle class, who stroll the colonnades and take their babies – or their financial newspapers – to rest with under the trees.

THE ARCHITECTURE OF THE ISLANDS If you want to know where the centre of Paris is, and perhaps also its most romantic part, look for its heart. The historic islands of the city floating gently on the Seine – the Île de la Cité and Île Saint-Louis – are the city's historic and geographic centre, but they're also where you'll discover the soul of *le vieux* Paris – the old Paris; the soft, sentimental Paris of centuries past, rather than the sharp-edged Paris of the present and future. Connected to the rest of Paris by various highly photogenic bridges, the islands with their intimate and evocative villages are still considered a little 'set apart' from the city by those who live there. In fact, their inhabitants, who have included such luminaries as Proust, Hemingway, Helena Rubinstein and former president Georges Pompidou, like to think of themselves as being a little special – some stores even charge for delivery *sur le continent*, arguing that Paris – the Paris outside of their own – is 'another world'. It's easy to see why they are filled with pride. The honey-coloured 17th-century buildings represent architecture of the most harmonious kind, while the quiet side streets offer picture-postcard views of the city and the Seine on either side. It's Paris as visitors imagine it: magical, historical, beautiful, memorable.

THE ARCHITECTURE OF COLOUR Newly arrived visitors to Paris may surmise that the city is one without a love of colour. Unlike, say, Mexico or Cuzsco, Paris is constructed primarily of beiges, greys and that very Parisian shade of taupe (some people like to call it 'greige'). Much of the architecture is a firm off-white while even the interiors veer towards elegant, understated shades. But look closely and you'll see that Paris has a passion for hues just like any other place: they simply show it in quieter ways. In fact, once you start to notice all the dramatic shades, you'll see that they seem more intense because of the backdrop of neutrals. Three of the most dominant colours are red, mauve and green, which show up in curious places, such as macaroons, Metro signs and hotel foyers. Red is a particular favourite of Paris, especially the strong, rich saturated red. It can be seen in the city's interiors, in the cakes, especially those containing framboise, fraise and cerise, and also in places such as Hediard, where red (the store's brand colour) engulfs you the moment you enter the place. Mauve is also favoured by many people (as is its offshoot, pink), and particularly loved by patisseries and bistros (many cafés even buy their woven chairs in pretty purple shades). But perhaps the most vibrant of Paris's colours is green. All of Paris is in love with green. A soft, almost indescribable mix of apple green, mint green, celadon green and pea green (or perhaps it is shades of all of them), Paris green has been around for centuries. It is perhaps most famous for being the signature shade of the much-loved patisserie Ladurée (just as pale blue is with Tiffany jewellers), but it is also seen often in interiors, fashion, floral and window displays, cakes, drinks and even homewares (it also goes well with beige and grey).

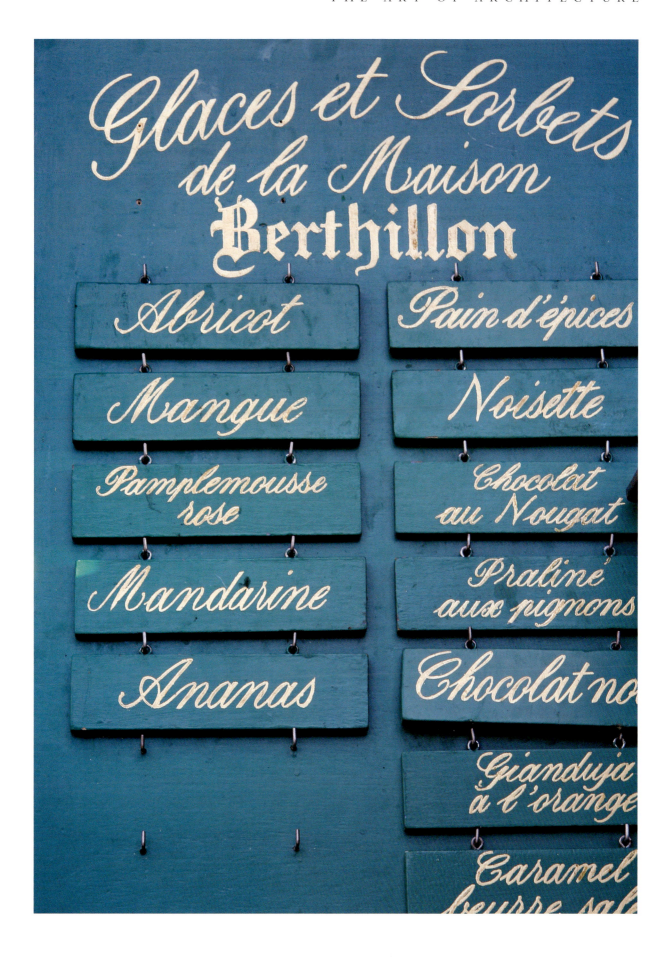

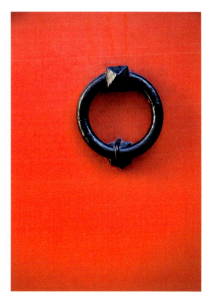
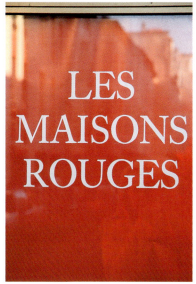

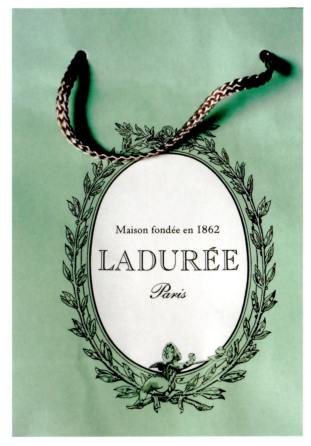

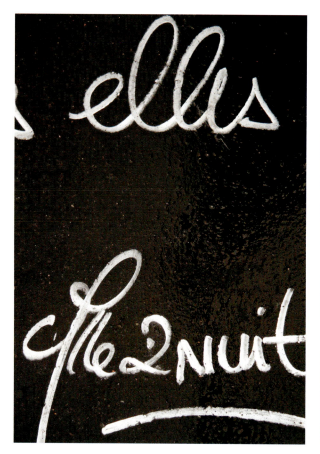

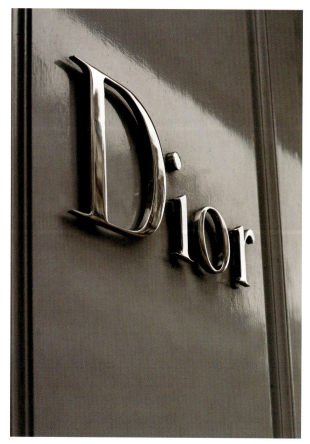

INTERIORS

'If I were to be the ruler of France, I would want to make Paris not only the most beautiful city in the world, that the world has ever known, but the most beautiful city that could ever be.'

– Napoleon Bonaparte

Architecture is not the only area in which the French take great pride in their aesthetics. Venture inside many Parisian homes and hotels, and you'll find interiors that reflect style, glamour, an intriguing eclecticism and an unerring sense of good taste. For Parisians, an interior is not just an interior, a place to go where the cafés and parks are closed; it is a space to impart their personal style, a well-defined sanctuary from the madness of life and the chaos of the city. Parisians are so fastidious about their private spaces; they even make jokes about their obsessive perfection with *la bonne table* and just about everything else in the home. There are two well-known sayings that describe the French flair for orchestrating a stylish life – *joie de vivre* – joy of life – and *savoir-faire*. The second is perhaps more pertinent, however, because 'joie' rarely comes into the equation. For the French, having a sense of style is a very serious business.

This preoccupation with design and the decorative arts has always been part of the French mindset. Just look at the château of Versailles. The decadent opulence of this grand palace is, of course, legendary. But the tradition of decorating goes back centuries, to even before Louis XVI built Marie Antoinette a Neo-Classical *folie*, complete with grotto and imaginary cows. Even Napoleon had an obsession with porcelain – when the French leader was banished to St Helena in 1815, he apparently demanded that his favourite plates went with him, not to use, but to take down and look at when he felt particularly melancholy.

Such is the French talent for creating an interior that their influence on design is now felt worldwide. In fact, it could be argued that the French have perhaps done more for interiors than any other nationality. French designers and fabric manufacturers are certainly some of the most famous names in the design world – think of Philippe Starck, Christian Liaigre, Frédéric Méchiche, Madame Castaing, Jacques Garcia, Andrée Putman and Catherine Memmi. Many of these names, including Starck and Méchiche, have been so successful, they've now ventured beyond the home into hotels and household objects. In fact, many hotels, such as the Hôtel Le A and Trocadéro Dokhan in Paris, and the Delano, Mondrian, Royalty and Hudson hotels in America now market the fact that they have been 'done' by these designers as much as they do their soft pillows and efficient business facilities.

Some of the predominant French 'looks' include the following:

French Empire: A style dictated by proportion, order and harmony that was largely influenced by Napoleon Bonaparte but was also fuelled by the emerging middle class's desire for luxury.

Louis XV: At one stage seen in virtually every bourgeois home from Paris to Toorak, Melbourne, the Louis XV look focuses on lots of curves. The more curves, the better.

Provence: Almost as ubiquitous as the Louis XV and Louis XVI looks, the Provence style is based on layer upon layer of pale shades – creams, off-whites and stone tones – with lots of country references: copper pans, plump cushions, linen-covered couches, stone floors, French doors and big dogs.

Folie: A surprisingly popular look, at least in Paris, and one that is gaining popularity across the design globe, the 'folie' style hints at eclecticism but is much more than that. It's about mixing and matching looks, while keeping one eye on the clutter. It's offbeat, original, highly individual, and loved by people because it allows for personality to show through in a room. It's about pairing a set of Arne Jacobsen's 'Series 7' chairs with a Murano chandelier and retro lamps and making it all look absolutely fabulous.

Black and white: Reflecting classic elegance with a modern kick, the monochrome look has become extremely fashionable in recent years, although designer Frédéric Méchiche has been practicing it for the past decade. (His designs for the Hôtel Le A and Trocadéro Dokhan's in Paris are pure monochromatic glamour.) Although Méchiche loves crisp, defined black and white stripes, the latest look is to use the two tones in an almost Baroque fashion – basically, anything goes.

Rothschild: More of a 'put down' than a design style, it is nevertheless prevalent in many newly wealthy homes, and is a mix (some call it a mish-mash) of styles. Think of African art mixed with Art Deco, Directoire, Empire, Renaissance, Gothic, Louis XV and Louis XVI, then enhanced with a whole lot of gilt and antiques. Or just think of the Hearst mansion at San Simeon. And then exaggerate it.

Flea market: The French are indefatigable foragers, and this penchant for perusing the flea markets quite often shows up in the style of their homes. The French love a find, and more so if it's a beautifully made *objet d'art.*

Particularly unusual pieces are often showcased on the fireplace mantelpiece; others are relegated to vignette-style collections of *objets trouvés* scattered around the rooms. It's the unpredictability of it that the French love – that, and the sheer whimsy of it all.

Colour: Many people believe the French don't understand colour, that they prefer beige, taupe and grey. But this isn't true. The French love a splash of colour as much as the next person. Just go to Ladurée to see how they play with beautiful shades. Some of the more elegant French tones include Pompadour pink, a saturated pale raspberry shade beloved by the legendary Madame, as well as Empress Eugénie and Marie Antoinette; pea green, versions of which are found all over Paris, including in Ladurée's branding (it's virtually a staple of French interior decoration); lilac, which is also seen all over Paris in myriad shades; red, another much-loved favourite of the French for its dramatic glamour; French blue, which is a cross between powder blue and mauve, and Prussian blue, a favourite of Napoleon that's more of a deep, refined, almost porcelain blue. The French don't normally mix these colours – that would be too extravagant – but rather focus on one, and then decorate the space around it.

Photography supplied courtesy of Château les Merles (www.lesmerles.com)
Photography by Stephen Clement

A SENSE OF CLASSIC PARIS While Parisian interiors generally waver between Louis XV, Empire, folie, minimalist, modern or flea market chic, there is another timeless look that can be found in many elegant homes and hotels throughout the city – that of 'classic Paris'. Classic Paris is, just as its name sounds, a gentle style of decorating that neither upsets nor offends nor pushes the upholstery buttons (and then deliberately puts them in the wrong place). It is an attempt at pure sophistication, and most of the time it succeeds. Drawing on classic French colours, including cherry red, and deep Parisian greens, it employs a great deal of silk, swathes of dramatic curtains, clipped topiary trees, walls of ivy, a sunroom that looks out to a pretty garden, grand paintings and perfectly matched furniture, all of which fall into line in the most obedient way. Highly glamorous but also highly difficult to maintain unless you have a housekeeper and gardener to help, it's demanding decorating that, like a top French model, asks for a lot but then delivers the look beautifully. Le Bristol, the Hôtel des Marronniers (above and right) and Hôtel de l'Abbaye are all fine example of classic Paris style.

Hôtel Marronniers, on the Left Bank

Hôtel de l'Abbaye

Hôtel de l'Abbaye, Left Bank

Hôtel le Bristol, Right Bank

The gardens of the famous Hôtel le Bristol

A SENSE OF SOPHISTICATION Tucked away in the 16th arrondissement, a quietly elegant part of the city known for its *haute bourgeois* style and not much else, there is a hotel that looks like it might be a stuffy, buttoned up sort of place – the kind you'd find bored businessmen and even-more-bored wives – but venture inside and it's actually a flamboyant ode to French style at its most fabulously sophisticated. Designed by Frédéric Méchiche and beloved by the fashion set (Armani books out the entire hotel for all his staff each Fashion Week), the Hôtel Trocadéro Dokhan's, or Le Dokhan's, as it is known (pictured above, right and following pages) is the equivalent of a dress-up cupboard for grown-ups, only one owned by a very rich, very tasteful Parisian aunt. The interior of the elevator is covered in panels from an antique 1930s Louis Vuitton trunk (so that you feel as if you're rising between floors in a luxurious steamer trunk – which gives a whole new meaning to travel), the hall is decked out in bold black-and-white awning stripes, the sitting room shimmers with enormous handmade ecru silk curtains, like the interior equivalent of a carefully put together haute couture gown, the corners are filled with dainty mauve chairs, and the Champagne Bar – one of the most fabulous spaces in Paris – is covered in timber panelling the colour of absinthe-green and edged in gold leaf; a truly spectacular sight, especially at night when it's all lit by hundreds of candles. One journalist called the style 'early Neo-Classical bonbonnière', and it certainly shimmers with unexpected glamour. In short, it's the perfect Parisian mix: equal parts surprise, sentiment and style.

A SENSE OF FRENCH How to describe the quintessential French look? Ever so slightly different from both the 'Classic Paris' style (which uses lots of rich reds and/or Parisian greens) and the 'Grand' style, the 'French' look is one that relies more on subtlety, while still incorporating traditional French decorating elements. You've probably seen this look before – it's so popular that it's spread across the interior design globe, from South Kensington to Sydney and the Upper East Side.

So how do you recognise it? Well, look for the main elements – a cream or oatmeal colour base with a layering of classic French gold on top (mirrors, photo frames, candlesticks); stylish drapes in shades of pale gold, cream, French blue or stripes (and usually in taffeta-like fabrics); criss-cross parquetry floors; a fireplace (which is often the centrepiece); elegant couches or chaises in oatmeal, cream or soft colours and lots of plump cushions. There will also usually be high ceilings, chandeliers and French doors going out to a balcony or finely clipped garden. It may sound like a fussy space filled to the brim with French bits but in fact it's a look that quite often ends up being calm and even understated, thanks to the quiet colours and lovely proportions.

Photography supplied courtesy of Chez Vous. www.chezvous.com
Apartments available to rent through Chez Vous.

Photography supplied courtesy of Chez Vous. www.chezvous.com
Apartments available to rent through Chez Vous.

Photography supplied courtesy of Chez Vous. www.chezvous.com
Apartments available to rent through Chez Vous.

A SENSE OF WHIMSY Parisians love a little wit and whimsy in their decorating. It speaks of intelligence and humour, two things Parisians love in equal measure. Whimsy may show up in the use of colour (think of those places decorated in a rich shocking pink or ripe lime), in objects (think of things found in flea markets or country barns), or in a completely unexpected mix of decorating styles – a rusty old iron café chair arranged with the finest of architectural books on top of it, for example. In the last few years, the whimsical look has almost taken over the neo-Baroque one in popularity, at least with funky new hotels eager to set the scene and draw in jaded international travellers tired of the same old thing. Le General, for example, made a splash with the media when it first opened on a grubby side street in the Republic, especially because the candy colours didn't quite match the neighbourhood outside. Using pink, pink and more pink, with layers of vanilla-white between it all, it was sheer folly, but oh, so much fun. And then there is Christian Lacroix's take on whimsy, the Hôtel du Petit Moulin in the Marais; a fabulous fantasy of colour, form and surprise that feels like an after-hours playground for adults. Featuring a sitting room soaked in aubergine, a reception styled in almond,

green and raspberry, a bar/dining room decked out in primary reds and yellows, and other corners given over to polka dots and stripes, along with lashings of retro chairs, pop art touches and wild collages, it seems as if it shouldn't all fit together but somehow does. And its guests can't help but fall head-over-heels in love with it all. But perhaps the most celebrated example of new French whimsy is Oscar Wilde's old haunt, L'Hotel (below), on the sentimental Left Bank. Once a seedy, shabby dive, it has been given a new lease of life and turned into a hip hideaway for celebrities, media and designers looking for something different (Johnny Depp apparently loves it), thanks to a completely whimsical facelift. The circular stairwell, which stretches up the inside of the hotel to all of the rooms, was turned into a feature, with chandeliers, leopard-print carpet and arched picture windows that framed the curvaceous form of the stairs on all sides. The downstairs bar and dining area was given a theatrical makeover with acres of rich red velvet and more leopard-print carpet, while the cellar was turned into a Bedouin-style boudoir and pool. Sheer whimsy, of course, but now it's one of the most booked-out places in town.

L'Hotel on the Left Bank; an ode to whimsy

L'Hotel

Le General Hotel; where wit, whimsy and prettiness merge in a perfect French mix

The Hôtel du Petit Moulin was decorated by Christian Lacroix, and displays his signature flair

A SENSE OF SURPRISE Some Paris interiors are designed to tease, surprise and even shock as much as they do entertain and comfort. And I don't mean with the use of simple whimsy or a slightly unexpected mix of styles. I mean with the use of deliberate tactics. Like this 'cellar' dwelling, for example, (these pages and over) which was formerly the garbage disposal for a grand mansion in the Marais and then left to linger as a 'nothing' space when the building was converted to apartments. One of the residents spotted it one day, and knew it was destined for better things. Having already renovated homes in other parts of Paris as well as Marrakech, she had an eye and an instinct for spotting the potential in unusual (and unused) abodes, and immediately bought the space outright. Now, the cellar and its contents are as surprising as the space it's been carved out of. Entered via a set of stairs guarded by knight's armour ('he's our doorman for parties,' explains the owner, laughing), the apartment widens to a 'play area' featuring a spa bath – which guests have to step over to reach the rest of the place – a sauna and an ensuite, complete with wine cellar installed above the toilet. The principal living area, meanwhile, consists of a kitchen that's simply an enormous bar and an all-in-one entertainment space that includes leopard-print sofas, a bed and study area. 'It's the perfect place for entertaining,' says the owner, with a wink. It may well be the perfect pad for parties, but down here, beneath a beautifully arched ceiling that harks back to its cellar days, it's also a sanctuary from the street above. Eclectic, eccentric and completely ingenious, all at the same time.

Apartments available to rent through A la Carte Paris Apartments. www.alacarte-paris-apartments.com

Apartments available to rent through A la Carte Paris Apartments. www.alacarte-paris-apartments.com

A SENSE OF GRANDEUR Parisians love anything grand, be it a monument, a façade or simply a celebration. Nobody does grand, after all, quite like the French. When it comes to their homes, however, it's difficult to do grand properly – unless they're living in the right interior to begin with. Because of this passion for glamour and grandeur, many Parisians set their sights on buying one of the larger, high-ceilinged apartments or houses rather than the smaller studios or maid's quarters tucked under the mansard roofs. Featuring beautifully proportioned rooms, tall French windows and quite often their own private garden – a rarity indeed in Paris – these properties are coveted among the middle class, and for that reason are some of the most expensive in the city. This magnificent residence in the Marais is an example of a truly grand Parisian home, and is unusual in that it was originally one-half of an enormous mansion. The residence was formerly owned by two sisters, one of whom decided to 'cut' the property down the middle in jealous protest of her sibling's

love affair with a handsome politician. The beautiful sister's half was eventually sold to become a school. The jealous sister's half stayed a private residence, and changed hands many times before eventually falling into the possession of a woman with a passion for unusual architecture. The exterior façade is typical of a grand Parisian home, with ornate stonework and imposing windows that look out to a large garden. The interior, however, is slightly more unique, no doubt because of its origins. The principal room is a dramatic two-storey space made even more theatrical because of a mezzanine that cuts across it. Set over varying levels, the living spaces include a living room with an enormous glass chandelier, a dining room with modern chairs, a reading room, an entertainment area and a contemporary kitchen. One door leads out to the carriage yard; another to the magnificent garden. The space is even more unusual because it shows the stonework of the impressively thick walls, further adding to the sense of luxury and drama.

Apartments available to rent through A la Carte Paris Apartments. www.alacarte-paris-apartments.com

Apartments available to rent through A la Carte Paris Apartments. www.alacarte-paris-apartments.com

Apartments available to rent through A la Carte Paris Apartments. www.alacarte-paris-apartments.com

Apartments available to rent through A la Carte Paris Apartments. www.alacarte-paris-apartments.com

A SENSE OF UNDERSTATEMENT Going against the design grain is just as popular a pastime as religiously following the tried and true French styles, and the neo-mono look is perhaps the best example of the French rebellious streak. Far from following the ornate decorating styles and dressing a room in a lot of silk and gilt, the neo-mono look takes everything away and then starts all over again. The result? Well, very little really, but that's the point, and it's so breathtakingly elegant in its simplicity you wonder why the French never considered it before. Take the Hôtel Le Sénat, for example, (above, and right) which is a boutique hideaway, right across from the Luxembourg gardens. It's difficult to find because the façade is so minimalist as to be nothing more than a gold plaque and a door, but inside you begin to get the picture. Decorated in the hotel's signature shade – pale grey – it uses bold, wide stripes to create dramatic patterns of form and shape. The hallway is like walking into a funfair ride while the rooms – decorated in grey and white with trimmings of black – are pared down to the point of being chic. It is so beautiful, you'll want to move in and never leave. And then there's the Hôtel Le A, which is just about one of the most delicious places you'll ever see, certainly in Paris. The result of collaboration between conceptual artist Fabrice Hybert and interior designer Frédéric Méchiche, it was one of the very first real 'design hotels' in the city and has been described as being less of a boutique hotel and more of a 'work of art'. Inspired by the shape of the Eiffel Tower (thus the 'A'), and also the name of the street it sits on (Artois), the hotel's branding and its rooms have a certain graphic simplicity that just murmurs style and sophistication. The downstairs reception and library are a slash of black while the bar and dining room are a whisper of white – a contrast of tones that results in pure architectural poetry. There's even a sitting area graced with more than 300 books on design and fashion should you want to be further inspired. The upstairs rooms, meanwhile, are an irresistible swish of marle grey and white, and so beautiful, most guests immediately wish they were better dressed. A fair few of them are, since the hotel is beloved by models, stylists, photographers and magazine editors, particularly during Fashion Week. A place where pure minimalism meets maximum glamour, the hotel is now leading the way in design hideaways. To use a well-worn cliché, Le A is *ooh la la*.

Hôtel Le Sénat

Hôtel Le A

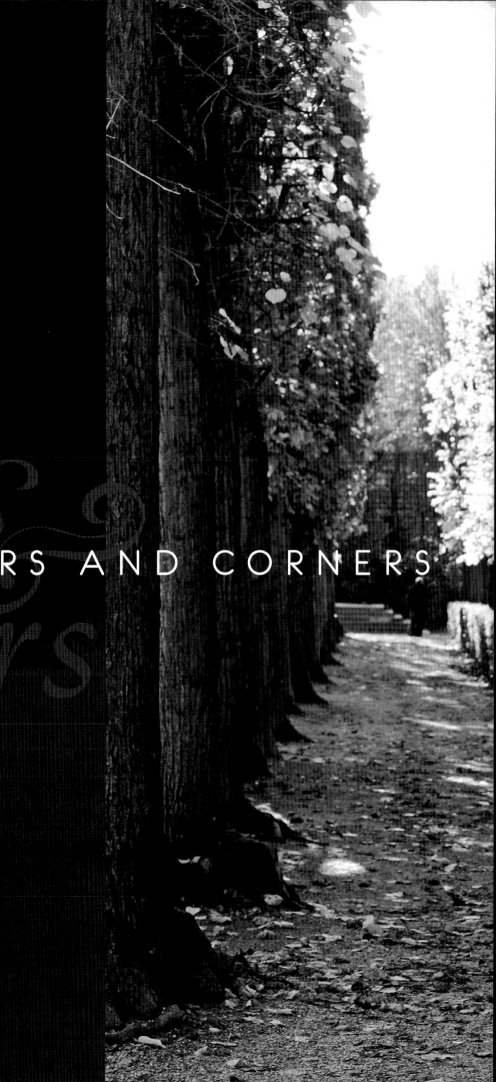

Paris is divided into 20 neighbourhoods called arrondissements. Many of these are known by their general name – the Marais, Saint-Germain, and so on – but they are also recognized by their corresponding number, which is the same one used to identify them in the Paris postal service – such as the sixth, the seventh, the first, the fourth, and so on … (although in French these are written as 5ème and 6ème). Each of these neighbourhoods has its particular personality, character and atmosphere. The Marais, for example, is regarded as being a haven of bohemian style; a lively enclave of buzzing shops, cafés, winding side streets and sights with a strong alternative lifestyle. The Latin Quarter is similarly rich in bohemian spirit, but tends to be more occupied with students and writers. The neighbourhood around the Boulevard Saint-Germain, on the other hand, was once firmly boho – intellectuals, philosophers and writers such as Hemingway and Fitzgerald frequented these streets – but it now veers determinedly towards bourgeois, although many of the city's publishing houses are still based here. And the next neighbourhood along, the 7ème, which sits in the shadow of the Eiffel Tower, is just as gentrified, and perhaps even wealthier than the famous sixth before it, but has its own quiet understated style. Other arrondissements reflect different characters, different spirits. But all are worth seeing, and exploring, and experiencing just once, if not several times more.

What few visitors to Paris realise, however, is that inside these arrondissements, there are smaller, more intimate quartiers, which are just as atmospheric, and perhaps easier to experience. Each arrondissement has four quartiers, and quite often each quartier is slightly different from the one beside it. So within the sixth, for example, there is Odéon, Saint-Germain-des-Prés, Monnaie and Notre-Dame-des-Champs – each a little distinct from the other. Clued-up visitors take an entire afternoon to see a single quartier, revelling in its history, its atmosphere, its beauty, its various moods during different moments of the day, and even its local characters, who can be discovered in its various cafés, bistros, patisseries and stores. It's one of the best ways to explore Paris, and allows you to really become intimate with the city, and not just glaze over it as swarms of tourists do.

Another way to get to know the city better is to seek its greener corners. Paris may be famous for its monuments and icons, but it's also known for the serenity and beauty that can be found in its many peaceful parks, gardens, squares, courtyards and enclaves. Indeed, some argue that it is these latter places, with their unexpected pleasures, that really make Paris what it is. It's difficult to convey just how lovely Paris's parks and gardens are, especially when the light filters through the branches of the trees, someone walks by and nods 'bonjour' in greeting and the scene starts to magically resemble an old-fashioned postcard.

The Parisians have a phrase to describe these little things: *petit tresors*, which literally means 'the small treasures' of life. It refers to the tucked-away bouffe de bistro where you like to have a beef bourguignon; that secret garden you like to visit at lunchtime; those stallholders you come to know at your favourite street market and revisit every other day, just to say 'bonjour'; that special table you like to sip a glass of Domaine Griottes at on Thursdays; that Île Saint-Louis bridge you like to detour over on your walk home.

Most people, after a period of time in Paris, discover their own *petit tresors*: treasures so precious they sear themselves into the subconsciousness and remain there, in the recesses of the memory, for a lifetime.

Here are just a few to start your Parisian experience. We've only provided a selection, because Paris is all about promise: the idea that you might find something – some memorable place, corner, café, store or experience – that few other people have discovered. Paris has its architecture, interiors and style, but it's the unexpected pleasures that make this place truly special.

GARDENS, GRAND AND SMALL It may not seem like it, but Paris is a gardener's city. Unlike London or Melbourne, it doesn't demonstrate this fondness for foliage in an overt way, by planning the inner city around enormous parks and petite neighbourhood gardens, although it does have its share of grand green spaces. Rather, Paris prefers to place its gardens so that you come across them unexpectedly, while stumbling out of the Louvre (as in the Tuileries), or after a wander through the area bordered by Boulevard Saint-Germain and Place St-Sulpice side streets (as in the Luxembourg Gardens), or even while walking to the Eiffel Tower (the gardens of the Rodin Museum). In the following pages are some of the gardens you may come across on a stroll through Paris, from the majestic Luxembourg Gardens to the sublime, divine Jardins de Babylone and the smaller gardens scattered throughout the greenery of Paris.

Gardens of the Rodin Museum

(These pages and over) Luxembourg Gardens

Luxembourg Gardens

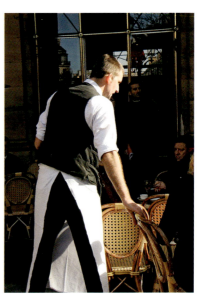

TABLES TO SIT AND THINK If there is one thing that visitors remember when they come to Paris, it is sitting at a café table, watching the city stroll by. Paris's cafés range marvellously in mood, from the philosophical seriousness of the Café de Flore, which has long been a haven for thinkers, writers and those who just love to take it all in, to the luscious Ladurée, which offers pastries to match its pretty interior. Some places envelop the visitor in gilded sumptuousness; others offer humble zinc counter-and-blackboard menu comfort. But whether your taste ventures towards fabulous or classic, one thing is certain: Paris is disproportionately blessed with places in which you can while away the afternoon.

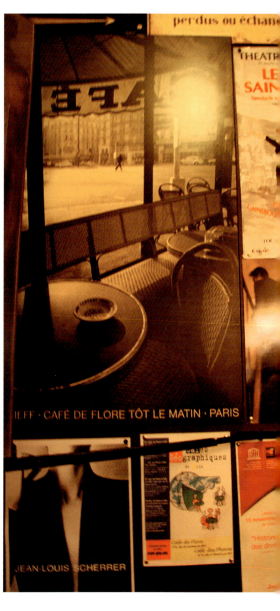

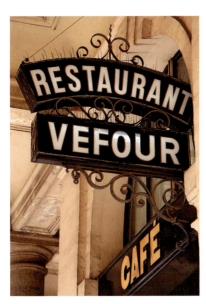

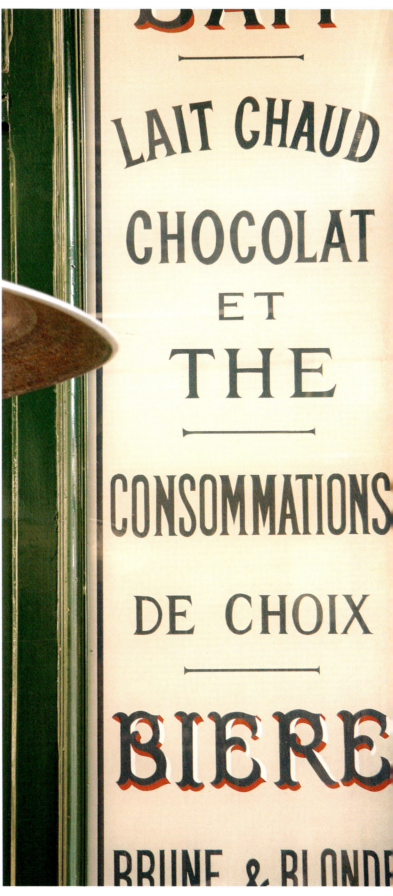

LAIT CHAUD
CHOCOLAT
ET
THE
CONSOMMATIONS
DE CHOIX
BIERE
BRUNE & BLONDE

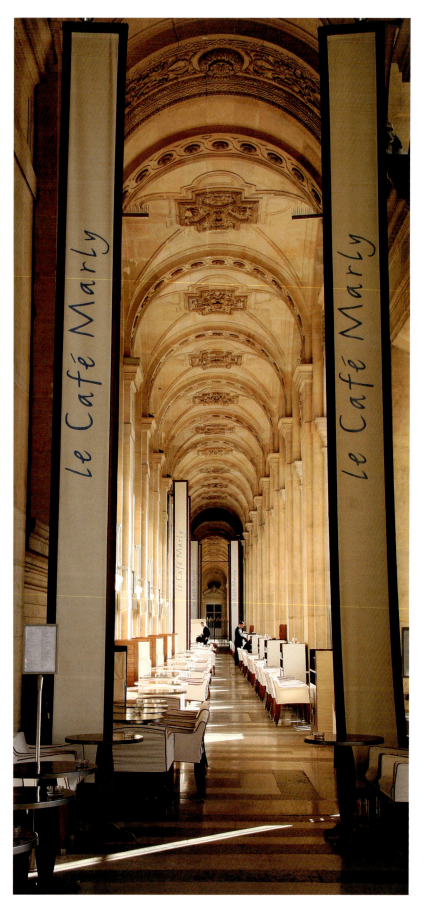

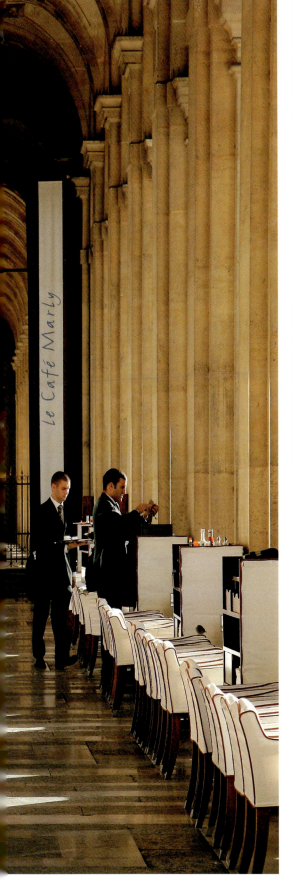

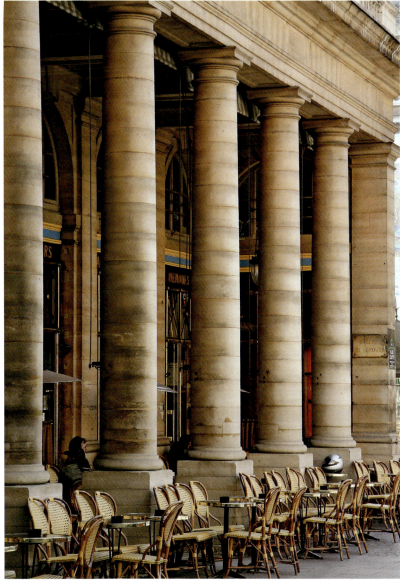

Le Comptoir Right Bank

188 SIDE STREETS TO GET LOST IN Paris is famous for its grand boulevards and majestic thoroughfares, but it's also renowned for having some of the most enchanting side streets in Europe. You only have to walk through the Left Bank to see glimpses of tiny, winding pathways, mysterious steps to even more mysterious roads and cul-de-sacs that end in astonishingly beautiful Parisian scenes. In fact, some of the best experiences in Paris can be found by deliberately losing yourself for an afternoon and venturing off the beaten tourist track. It's only be being a '*flâneur*' – an aimless idler who wanders through the city in search of its soul – that you'll truly discover Paris, and make those singular finds that will stay with you forever. Some of the most beautiful side streets can be found on the Île Saint-Louis and Île de la Cité (see over), the Marais, and in the area around Boulevard Saint-Germain. This last section is literally crisscrossed with exquisite side streets, many of them so picture-perfect that they could almost be Parisian postcards come to life.

CORNERS TO DISCOVER The city's side streets are not the only places to lose yourself for a little while. Paris has some of the world's most enthralling stores, ranging from grand department stores to exquisite patisseries, irresistible flower shops, sublime fashion boutiques, divine bakeries and even endearingly small booksellers that line the Seine. It's also famous for its tempting bistros, restaurants and cafés. And then, of course, there are unexpectedly gorgeous corners, such as those hidden within its gracious churches, or those discovered within its whimsical children's playgrounds, many of which are scattered through Paris's parks and gardens. Whatever moves, delights or excites you, you can be sure you'll find it in Paris.

Photography courtesy of Jenny Wiederman

PLACES OUT OF TOWN When you need a break from the pace of Paris, the regions surrounding the city are well worth visiting. Not only are they just as beautiful as Paris, but they also offer a respite from the intensity of the city and its aesthetic riches. The quiet country villages offer charming markets to buy bags of produce at, not to mention photogenic scenes of French life, while the grander places, such as Château de Villandry, Versailles and Château les Merles (see over) offer an extraordinary glimpse into France's past. Whether it's gardens, architecture, gourmet food or simply style you're after, France's countryside has it all.

The impressive parterre of Château de Villandry

The famous gardens of Versailles

The style of Versailles

The understated glamour of Château les Merles

Photography supplied courtesy of Château les Merles (www.lesmerles.com)
Photography by Stephen Clement

Photography supplied courtesy of Château les Merles (www.lesmerles.com)
Photography by Stephen Clement

Photography supplied courtesy of Château les Merles (www.lesmerles.com)
Photography by Stephen Clement

Photography supplied courtesy of Château les Merles (www.lesmerles.com)
Photography by Stephen Clement

FEATURED HOTELS – PARIS AND SURROUNDS

Château les Merles Tuilières, 24520 Mouleydier. Phone +33 553 63 13 42. www.lesmerles.com

Hôtel de 'lAbbaye 10 rue Cassette, 75006, Paris. Phone +33 (0) 1 45 44 38 11. www.hotelabbayeparis.com

Hôtel du Petit Moulin 29/31 rue du Poitou, 75003, Paris. Phone +33 (0) 1 42 74 10 10.
    www.paris-hotel-petitmoulin.com

Hôtel Le A 4 rue d'Artois, 75008, Paris. Phone +33(0) 1 42 56 99 99. www.paris-hotel-a.com

Hôtel le Sénat 10 rue de Vaugirard, Paris. Phone +33 (0) 1 70 619 002. www.hotel-lesenat.com

Hôtel Marronniers 21 rue Jacob, 75006, Paris. Phone +33 (0) 1 43 25 30 60. www.hotel-marronniers.com

Le Bristol II2, rue du Faubourg St Honoré, 75008, Paris. Phone +33 (0) 1 53 43 43 00.
    www.hotel-bristol.com

Le General 5/7, rue Rampon, 75011 Paris. Phone +33 (0) 1 47 00 41 57. www.legeneralhotel.com

L'Hotel 13 rue Beaux Arts, 75006, Paris. Phone +33 (0) 1 44 41 99 00. www.l-hotel.com

Trocadéro Dokhan's 117 rue Lauriston, 75116, Paris. Phone +33 (0) 1 53 65 66 99. www.sofitel.com

APARTMENTS FOR RENT, PARIS

A la Carte Paris Apartments 4 rue Martel, 75010, Paris. Phone +33 (0) 1 42 46 42 57.
    www.alacarte-paris-apartments.com

Chez Vous 1001 Bridgeway, PMB 245, Sausalito, California, 94965, USA. Phone + 1 415 331 2535.
    www.chezvous.com

Paris Luxury Rentals Phone +1 415 850 5370. www.parisluxuryrentals.com

PHOTOGRAPHY CREDITS

Photographs of Château les Merles supplied courtesy of Château les Merles. Photographs by Stephen Clement. www.lesmerles.com

Photographs of Chez Vous apartment supplied courtesy of Chez Vous. www.chezvous.com

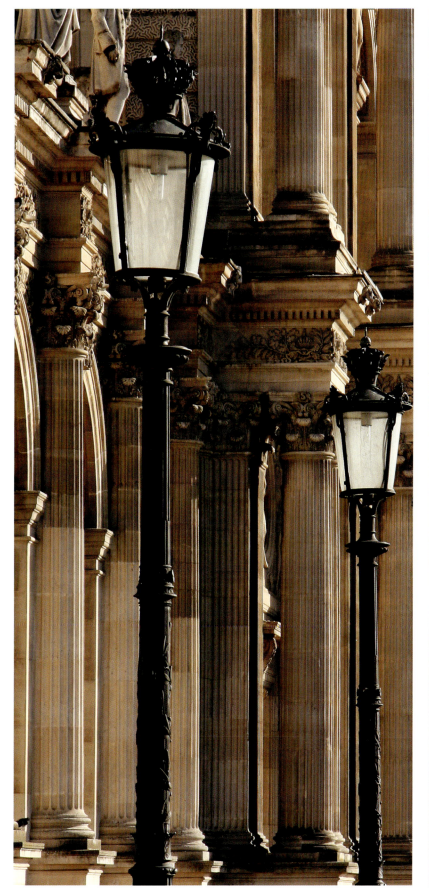
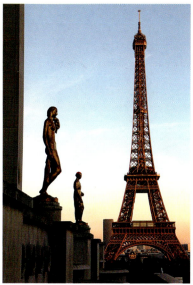